I am only one. But still,
I am one. I cannot do
everything, but still
I can do something. And
because I cannot do
everything, I will not
refuse to do the
something that I can do.

EDWARD EVERETT HALE
A 2ND HELPING OF CHICKEN SOUP FOR THE SOUL

The best and most
beautiful things in the
world cannot be seen or
even touched. They must
be felt with the heart.

HELEN KELLER

A 2ND HELPING OF CHICKEN SOUP FOR THE SOUL

The dynamics that are required to make any relationship work: Just keep putting your love out there.

ANONYMOUS

The most notable winners
usually encountered
heart-breaking obstacles
before they triumphed.
They won because they
refused to become
discouraged by
their defeats.

B. C. FORBES

A 2ND HELPING OF CHICKEN SOUP FOR THE SOUL

Being considerate of others will take [you] further in life than any college degree.

MARIAN WRIGHT EDELMAN
A CUP OF CHICKEN SOUP FOR THE SOUL

The greatest happiness
in life is the conviction
that we are loved.

VICTOR HUGO
CHICKEN SOUP FOR THE COUNTRY SOUL

A friend is a gift
you give yourself.

ROBERT LOUIS STEVENSON
CHICKEN SOUP FOR THE TEENAGE SOUL

Three things in the human life are important: The first is to be kind. The second is to be kind. And the third is to be kind.

HENRY JAMES
A 4TH COURSE OF CHICKEN SOUP FOR THE SOUL

First say to yourself
what you would be;
and then do what
you have to do.

EPICTETUS
CHICKEN SOUP FOR THE TEENAGE SOUL

Hoping means seeing that the outcome you want is possible, and then working for it.

DR. BERNIE S. SIEGEL
CHICKEN SOUP FOR THE SURVIVING SOUL

The only genuine love
worthy of the name is
unconditional.

JOHN POWELL
CHICKEN SOUP FOR THE MOTHER'S SOUL

A single grateful
thought raised to
Heaven is the
most perfect prayer.

GOTTHOLD EPHRAIM LESSING

A 5TH PORTION OF CHICKEN SOUP FOR THE SOUL

The human spirit
cannot be paralyzed.
If you are breathing,
you can dream.

MIKE BROWN
A 4TH COURSE OF CHICKEN SOUP FOR THE SOUL

The greatest gift is
a portion of thyself.

RALPH WALDO EMERSON
CHICKEN SOUP FOR THE TEENAGE SOUL

When you believe you can—you can!

MAXWELL MALTZ

A 4TH COURSE OF CHICKEN SOUP FOR THE SOUL

Let us outdo each other
in being helpful and
kind to each other
and in doing good.

HEBREWS 10:24 TLB

CHICKEN SOUP FOR THE CHRISTIAN SOUL

He who has a why
to live for can have
almost any how.

FRIEDRICH NIETZSCHE
A 4TH COURSE OF CHICKEN SOUP FOR THE SOUL

May the road rise to meet you, may the wind be always at your back, the sun shine warm upon your face, the rain fall soft upon your fields, and until we meet again, may God hold you in the palm of His hand.

IRISH BLESSING
CHICKEN SOUP FOR THE CHRISTIAN SOUL

To every thing there is a season, and a time to every purpose under the heaven: A time to be born, and a time to die.... A time to weep, and a time to laugh.

ECCLESIASTES 3:1-2,4 KJV

CHICKEN SOUP FOR THE CHRISTIAN SOUL

Everybody can be great...because anybody can serve. You don't have to have a college degree to serve.... You only need a heart full of grace. A soul generated by love.

DR. MARTIN LUTHER KING, JR.

CHICKEN SOUP FOR THE SOUL

Friendship is the golden thread that ties the heart of all the world.

JOHN EVELYN
A CUP OF CHICKEN SOUP FOR THE SOUL

And all the loveliest
things there be,
come simply so,
it seems to me.

EDNA ST. VINCENT MILLAY
CHICKEN SOUP FOR THE WOMAN'S SOUL

What's important in life is how we treat each other.

HANA IVANHOE, AGE 15
CHICKEN SOUP FOR THE TEENAGE SOUL

Love is the emblem of eternity; it confounds all notion of time.

ANNA LOUISE DE STAËL
CHICKEN SOUP FOR THE WOMAN'S SOUL

Kindness is in our power, even when fondness is not.

SAMUEL JACKSON
CHICKEN SOUP FOR THE CHRISTIAN SOUL

You must live in the present to secure your future.

REVEREND ROBERT CRAIG

CHICKEN SOUP FOR THE SURVIVING SOUL

If you judge people
you have no time
to love them.

MOTHER TERESA
CHICKEN SOUP FOR THE TEENAGE SOUL

Reach high, for stars lie hidden in your soul. Dream deep, for every dream precedes the goal.

PAMELA VAULL STARR
CHICKEN SOUP FOR THE WOMAN'S SOUL

Don't worry about failure. Worry about the chances you miss when you don't even try.

ANONYMOUS
CHICKEN SOUP FOR THE SOUL

Nobody has ever
measured, not even
poets, how much
the heart can hold.

ZELDA FITZGERALD
CHICKEN SOUP FOR THE WOMAN'S SOUL

Simple pleasures bring great happiness.

MARY HELEN BRINDELL
CHICKEN SOUP FOR THE SURVIVING SOUL

Kind words can be
short and easy to
speak, but their echoes
are truly endless.

MOTHER TERESA
CHICKEN SOUP FOR THE WOMAN'S SOUL

Life isn't a matter
of milestones
but of moments.

ROSE KENNEDY
CHICKEN SOUP FOR THE WOMAN'S SOUL

The love we give away
is the only love we keep.

ELBERT HUBBARD
CHICKEN SOUP FOR THE WOMAN'S SOUL

It takes a lot of understanding, time and trust to gain a close friendship.... As I approach a time in my life of complete uncertainty, my friends are my most precious asset.

ERYNN MILLER, AGE 18
CHICKEN SOUP FOR THE TEENAGE SOUL

There are two ways of spreading light: To be the candle or the mirror that reflects it.

EDITH WHARTON
A CUP OF CHICKEN SOUP FOR THE SOUL

When it comes down
to it, we all just
want to be loved.

JAMIE YELLIN, AGE 14
CHICKEN SOUP FOR THE TEENAGE SOUL

If you have one true
friend you have more
than your share.

THOMAS FULLER
A CUP OF CHICKEN SOUP FOR THE SOUL

It's kind of fun
to do the impossible!

WALT DISNEY
A CUP OF CHICKEN SOUP FOR THE SOUL

Make it a practice
to judge persons
and things in the
most favorable light
at all times,
in all circumstances.

ST. VINCENT DE PAUL,
CHICKEN SOUP FOR THE CHRISTIAN SOUL

Remember, we all stumble, everyone of us. That's why it's a comfort to go hand in hand.

EMILY KIMBROUGH
A CUP OF CHICKEN SOUP FOR THE SOUL

Love, true love, is
that which can give
the most without
asking or demanding
anything in return.

MAZIE HAMMOND
A 5TH PORTION OF CHICKEN SOUP FOR THE SOUL

A happy person is not a person in a certain set of circumstances, but rather a person with a certain set of attitudes.

HUGH DOWNS
A 2ND HELPING OF CHICKEN SOUP FOR THE SOUL

Faith is to believe what we do not see, and the reward of faith is to see what we believe.

AUGUSTINE

He has put his angels
in charge of you to
watch over you
wherever you go.

PSALM 91:11 NCV

The heart has reasons which reason cannot understand.

BLAISE PASCAL
CHICKEN SOUP FOR THE CHRISTIAN SOUL

Faith is believing in
things when common
sense tells you not to.

GEORGE SEATON

A CUP OF CHICKEN SOUP FOR THE SOUL

All that I have seen
teaches me to trust
the Creator for all
I have not seen.

RALPH WALDO EMERSON

CHICKEN SOUP FOR THE CHRISTIAN SOUL

The measure of a man's real character is what he would do if he knew he would never be found out.

T. B. MACAULAY
A CUP OF CHICKEN SOUP FOR THE SOUL

Hugging is an under-utilized resource with magical powers. When we open our hearts and arms, we encourage others to do the same. Think of the people in your life.... Please don't wait! Initiate!

CHARLES FARAONE
CHICKEN SOUP FOR THE SOUL

Obstacles are those frightful things you see when you take your eyes off your goal.

HENRY FORD
CHICKEN SOUP FOR THE SOUL

Great opportunities
to help others seldom
come, but small ones
surround us every day.

SALLY KOCH
CHICKEN SOUP FOR THE TEENAGE SOUL

Life is either a
daring adventure
or nothing at all.

HELEN KELLER
CHICKEN SOUP FOR THE WOMAN'S SOUL

Friends are there,
smile or tear.
Friends are there,
happiness or fear.
Friends are fun
and friends are clever,
And the ties that bind
friends will last forever.

HARMONY DAVIS, AGE 14
CHICKEN SOUP FOR THE KID'S SOUL

Keep away from people who try to belittle your ambitions. Small people always do that, but the really great people make you feel that you, too, can become great.

MARK TWAIN
A 2ND HELPING OF CHICKEN SOUP FOR THE SOUL

Do what you can
with what you have,
where you are.

THEODORE ROOSEVELT

CHICKEN SOUP FOR THE CHRISTIAN SOUL

The big question is
whether you are
going to be able
to say a hearty yes
to your adventure.

JOSEPH CAMPBELL
A 2ND HELPING OF CHICKEN SOUP FOR THE SOUL

There is no such thing as a self-made man. You will reach your goals only with the help of others.

GEORGE SHINN

A 5TH PORTION OF CHICKEN SOUP FOR THE SOUL

We are all pencils
in the hand of God.

MOTHER TERESA
A 2ND HELPING OF CHICKEN SOUP FOR THE SOUL

Laughter is essential
to our equilibrium,
to our well-being,
to our aliveness.

PETER MCWILLIAMS
CHICKEN SOUP FOR THE SURVIVING SOUL

Faith, Hope, Love.
You need all of
the above.

KRISTINE KIRSTEN
CHICKEN SOUP FOR THE SURVIVING SOUL

Blessed is the influence
of one true, loving
human soul on another.

GEORGE ELIOT
A 5TH PORTION OF CHICKEN SOUP FOR THE SOUL

There comes that mysterious meeting in life when someone acknowledges who we are and what we can be, igniting the circuits of our highest potential.

RUSTY BERKUS
A 2ND HELPING OF CHICKEN SOUP FOR THE SOUL

Do not worry about
your life...indeed your
heavenly Father knows
that you need
all these things.

MATTHEW 6:25,32 NRSV
CHICKEN SOUP FOR THE CHRISTIAN SOUL

The meaning of things lies not in the things themselves, but in our attitude towards them.

Antoine de Saint-Exupéry

A 3rd Serving of Chicken Soup for the Soul

You have to have faith
that there is a reason
you go through certain
things. I can't say I'm glad
to go through pain, but
in a way one must, in
order to gain courage
and really feel joy.

CAROL BURNETT

A 4TH COURSE OF CHICKEN SOUP FOR THE SOUL

The dedicated life
is the life worth living.

ANNIE DILLARD

A 3RD SERVING OF CHICKEN SOUP FOR THE SOUL

If we did all the things
we were capable of
doing, we would literally
astound ourselves.

THOMAS EDISON
A 4TH COURSE OF CHICKEN SOUP FOR THE SOUL

It is more blessed to
give than to receive.

ACTS 20:35 NCV

A 4TH COURSE OF CHICKEN SOUP FOR THE SOUL

We must not only
give what we have;
we must also give
what we are.

Désiré-Joseph Mercier

A 4th Course of Chicken Soup for the Soul

A thousand words will not leave so deep an impression as one deed.

HENRIK IBSEN
A 4TH COURSE OF CHICKEN SOUP FOR THE SOUL

The most permanent
lessons in morals are
those which come,
not of booky teaching,
but of experience.

MARK TWAIN

There's no such thing
as no chance.

HENRY FORD
CHICKEN SOUP FOR THE SURVIVING SOUL

Blessed are those
that can give without
remembering and take
without forgetting.

ELIZABETH BIBESCO

A 4TH COURSE OF CHICKEN SOUP FOR THE SOUL

Nothing is worth more
than this day.

GOETHE

A 5TH PORTION OF CHICKEN SOUP FOR THE SOUL

Don't live in anybody's
shadows or dreams.
If you have a dream,
act on it and it will
probably come true.

JUDY AND KATIE GRIFFLER
CHICKEN SOUP FOR THE SURVIVING SOUL

To cultivate kindness is
a valuable part of the
business of life.

SAMUEL JOHNSON
A 4TH COURSE OF CHICKEN SOUP FOR THE SOUL

The capacity to care
is the thing that gives
life its deepest meaning
and significance.

PABLO CASALS

That best portion
of a good man's life,
his little, nameless,
unremembered acts of
kindness and of love.

WILLIAM WORDSWORTH
A 2ND HELPING OF CHICKEN SOUP FOR THE SOUL

when you give of
yourself, you receive
more than you give.

ANTOINE DE SAINT-EXUPÉRY
A 4TH COURSE OF CHICKEN SOUP FOR THE SOUL

Hugging is the ideal gift...fun to give and receive, shows you care...and, of course, is fully returnable. Hugging is practically perfect. No batteries to wear out, inflation-proof, nonfattening, no monthly payments, theft-proof and nontaxable.

CHARLES FARAONE
CHICKEN SOUP FOR THE SOUL

Love is a wonderful
thing. You never have
to take it away from
one person to give it
to another. There's
always more than
enough to go around.

PAMELA J. deROY
A 4TH COURSE OF CHICKEN SOUP FOR THE SOUL

Most people are about
as happy as they make
up their minds to be.

ABRAHAM LINCOLN
A 2ND HELPING OF CHICKEN SOUP FOR THE SOUL

cherish your visions
and your dreams, as
they are the children
of your soul, the
blueprints of your
ultimate achievements.

NAPOLEON HILL
A 3RD SERVING OF CHICKEN SOUP FOR THE SOUL

Life is what we make it,
always has been,
always will be.

GRANDMA MOSES

A 2ND HELPING OF CHICKEN SOUP FOR THE SOUL

For everything you
have missed, you have
gained something else.

RALPH WALDO EMERSON
A 3RD SERVING OF CHICKEN SOUP FOR THE SOUL

Don't bug me.
Hug me!

BUMPER STICKER

CHICKEN SOUP FOR THE SOUL

Some people come into
our lives and quickly go.
Some stay for a while
and leave footprints
on our hearts and we
are never, ever the same.

ANONYMOUS
CHICKEN SOUP FOR THE TEENAGE SOUL

It's the action, not the fruit of the action, that's important. You have to do the right thing. It may not be in your power, may not be in your time, that there'll be any fruit. But that doesn't mean you stop doing the right thing. You may never know what results come from your action.

GANDHI

CHICKEN SOUP FOR THE SOUL

The Lord will watch
over your coming
and going both now
and forevermore.

PSALM 121:8 NIV

CHICKEN SOUP FOR THE CHRISTIAN SOUL

It is one of the most
beautiful compensations
of this life that no man
can sincerely try to
help another without
helping himself.

RALPH WALDO EMERSON
A 2ND HELPING OF CHICKEN SOUP FOR THE SOUL

Winning isn't always
finishing first.
Sometimes winning
is just finishing.

MANUEL DIOTTE
CHICKEN SOUP FOR THE SURVIVING SOUL

There are always two
choices, two paths
to take. One is easy.
And its only reward
is that it's easy.

ANONYMOUS
CHICKEN SOUP FOR THE TEENAGE SOUL

Life is a succession of lessons which must be lived to be understood.

HELEN KELLER

A 2ND HELPING OF CHICKEN SOUP FOR THE SOUL